I0815334

History of the Titanic

Finding the Titanic

by Julie Murray

Dash!
LEVELED READERS
An Imprint of Abdo Zoom • abdobooks.com

Level 1 – Beginning
Short and simple sentences with familiar words or patterns for children who are beginning to understand how letters and sounds go together.

Level 2 – Emerging
Longer words and sentences with more complex language patterns for readers who are practicing common words and letter sounds.

Level 3 – Transitional
More developed language and vocabulary for readers who are becoming more independent.

abdobooks.com

Published by Abdo Zoom, a division of ABDO, PO Box 398166, Minneapolis, Minnesota 55439.

Printed in the United States of America, North Mankato, Minnesota.
102024
012025

Photo Credits: Alamy, Getty Images, Newscom, Shutterstock
Production Contributors: Kenny Abdo, Jennie Forsberg, Grace Hansen, John Hansen
Design Contributors: Candice Keimig, Neil Klinepier

Library of Congress Control Number: 2024936543

Publisher's Cataloging in Publication Data

Names: Murray, Julie, author.
Title: Finding the Titanic / by Julie Murray
Description: Minneapolis, Minnesota : Abdo Zoom, 2025 | Series: History of the Titanic | Includes online resources and index.
Identifiers: ISBN 9781098287245 (lib. bdg.) | ISBN 9781098287948 (ebook) | ISBN 9781098288297 (Read-to-me ebook)
Subjects: LCSH: Underwater exploration--Juvenile literature. | Shipwrecks--North Atlantic Ocean-Juvenile literature. | Wrecks--Juvenile literature. | Historic ships--Juvenile literature. | Titanic (Steamship)--Juvenile literature.
Classification: DDC 910.9163--dc23

Table of Contents

Finding the Titanic

The **RMS** *Titanic* sunk on April 15, 1912. More than 1,500 lives were lost in the disaster.

Many people tried to locate the ship's wreckage. It took more than 70 years for one of these missions to be a success.

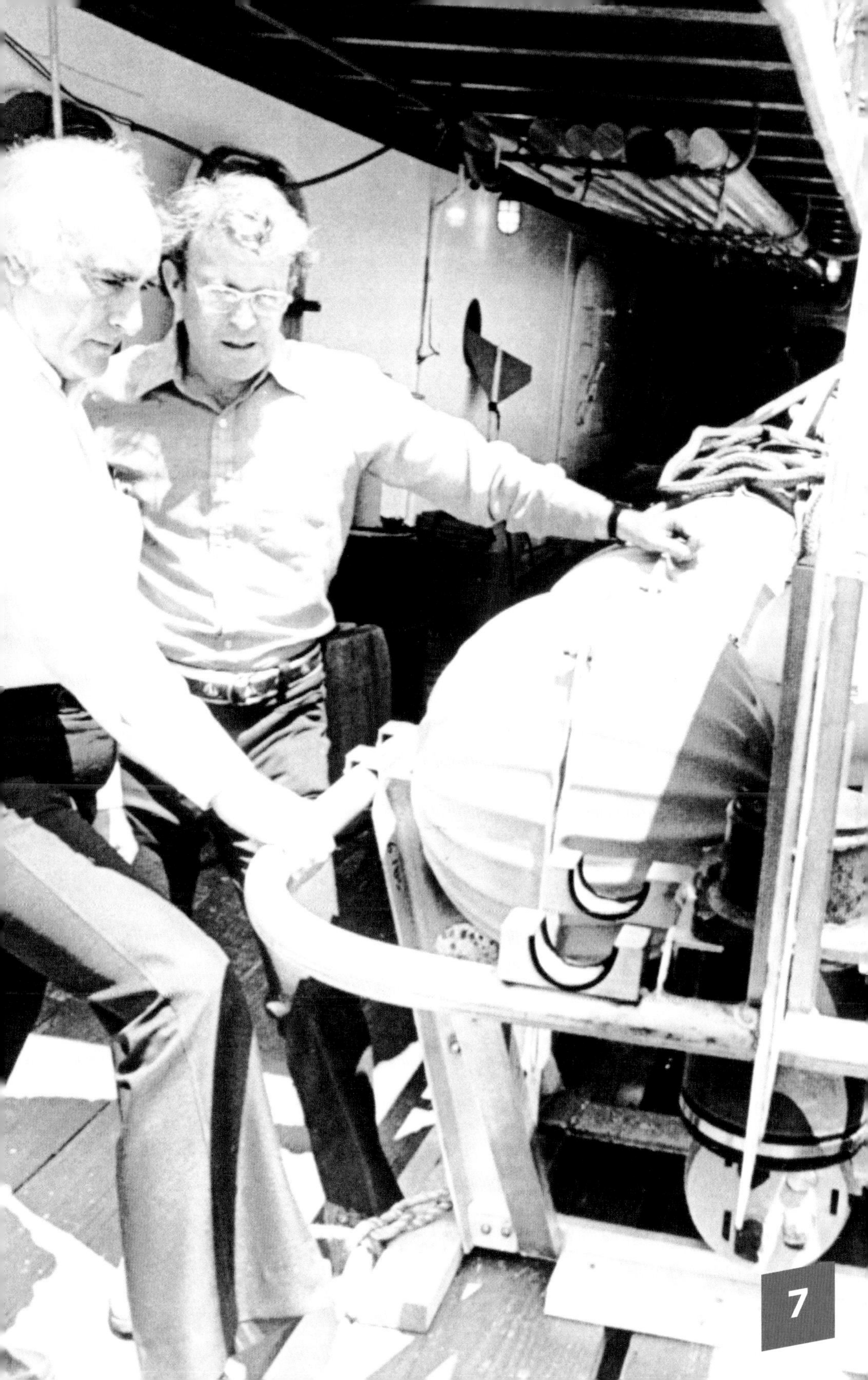

7

The Discovery

On September 1, 1985, Robert Ballard and his team located the *Titanic*.

The team found the ship deep in the Atlantic Ocean. It was 12,450 feet (3,795 m) below the ocean's surface.

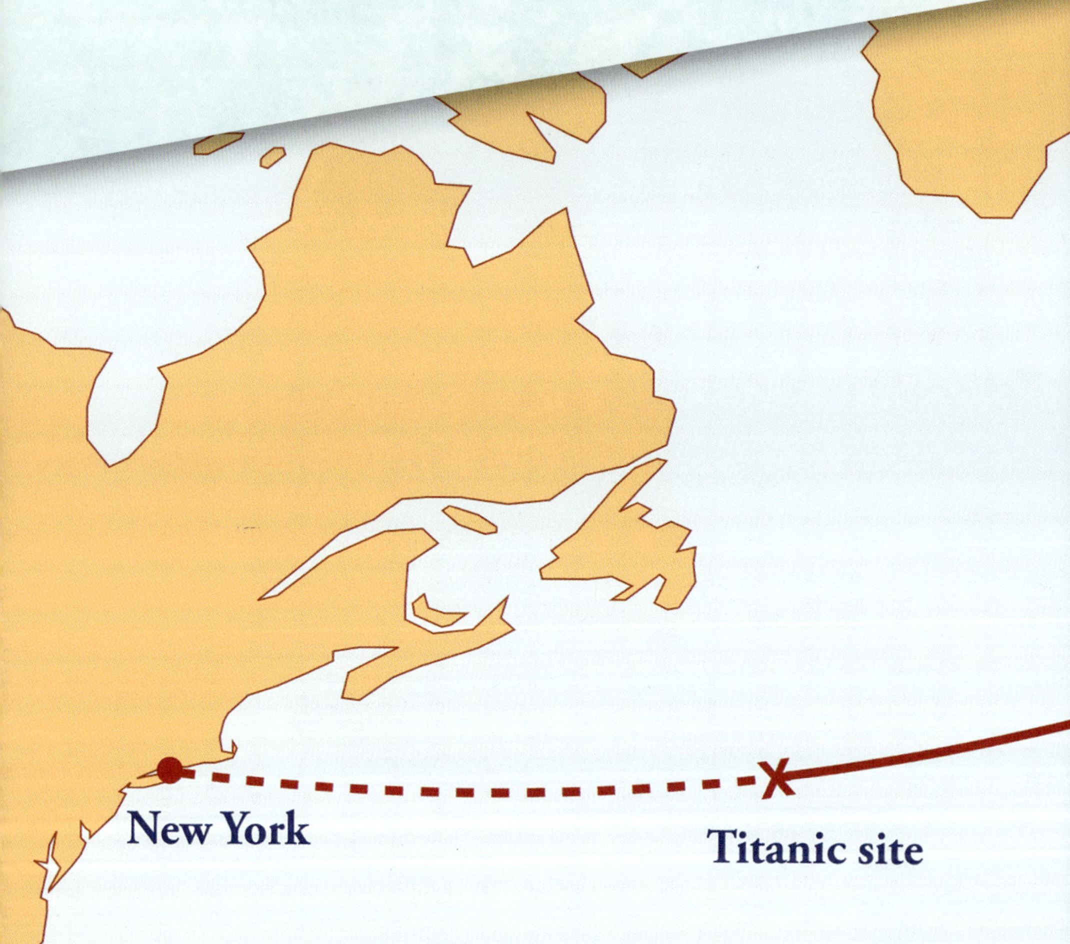

Queenstown
Southampton
Cherbourg
ATLANTIC
OCEAN

The team used **sonar** and a camera system called Argo to find the ship. One of the ship's **boilers** was the first thing to come into view.

Ballard returned to the site in 1986. He went down in a submarine. He used robots with cameras to capture detailed footage.

The footage showed what remained of the *Titanic's* grand staircase. It also revealed a large hole in the ship's **bow**.

Many others have visited the *Titanic* to explore the site. They have found and brought back thousands of **artifacts**.

In 2023, five people died attempting to visit the *Titanic* on the *Titan* submersible. The vessel **imploded** during decent.

More Facts

- Many people thought the *Titanic* sunk in one piece. It was discovered that the ship broke in half.
- The ship was found 400 miles (644 km) off the coast of Canada.
- The *Titanic's* **debris field** covers 15 square miles (39 sq km).

Glossary

artifact - any object made by human beings.

boiler - a closed pressure vessel that generates steam by heating water with thermal energy from burning fuel.

bow - the front part of a ship or boat.

debris field - an area where pieces of something that has been destroyed or broken down are scattered.

implode - to violently collapse or compress inward.

RMS - short for Royal Mail Ship.

sonar - a way to find objects underwater by sending and reflecting sound waves.

Index

Online Resources

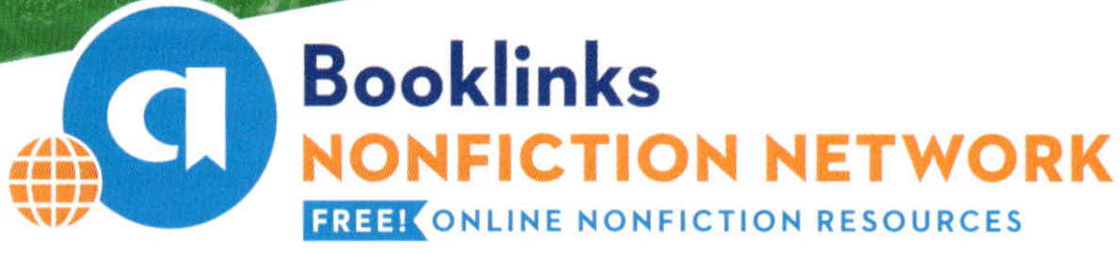

To learn more about finding the *Titanic*, please visit **abdobooklinks.com** or scan this QR code. These links are routinely monitored and updated to provide the most current information available.